# 365
# Thought-Provoking
# Questions for Boys
# Aged 15-17

# 365 Thought-Provoking Questions for Boys Aged 15-17

## One Question a Day for Personal Growth and Bolstering Identity

Aria Capri Publishing
Devon Abbruzzese
Mauricio Vasquez

Toronto, Canada

Authors:
Devon Abbruzzese
Mauricio Vasquez
Aria Capri Publishing

First Printing: May 2024

ISBN-978-1-998402-43-4 (Paperback book)
ISBN-978-1-998402-42-7 (Hardcover book)
ISBN-978-1-998402-41-0 (Electronic book)

# Introduction

In the tumultuous journey of adolescence, boys aged 15 to 17 find themselves at a crucial juncture where the questions they encounter can significantly influence their pathways to adulthood. As they navigate the complex landscape of middle adolescence, engaging them through thoughtful questions is not merely a way to pass the time but a fundamental strategy to foster growth, understanding, and connection. This book is designed to be a compass for those who guide these young men—parents, educators, and mentors—empowering them with a curated list of questions that touch on the core aspects of adolescent life and development.

## The Role of Inquiry in Adolescent Development

Adolescence is marked by rapid physical, emotional, and cognitive changes. At this stage, boys are forging identities, establishing independence, and exploring their values and beliefs. It is a time filled with challenges and opportunities, where the right questions can open doors to deeper self-awareness and introspection. Engaging adolescents with meaningful questions encourages them to reflect on their experiences, articulate their thoughts and feelings, and consider their future with greater clarity and purpose.

Questions are the keys that unlock the internal dialogues crucial for developing critical thinking and emotional intelligence. When we present adolescents with questions that challenge their perspectives or invite them to solve problems, we are not just asking them to think—we encourage them to learn how to think. This process is vital in cultivating a mindset equipped to tackle academic challenges and personal dilemmas.

## Strengthening Relationships Through Dialogue

For parents and caregivers, questions bridge adolescents' inner worlds. In a phase of life where communication gaps can widen, thoughtfully crafted questions help maintain and strengthen bonds. They signal interest, foster mutual respect, and open lines of communication, allowing adults to understand their teenage sons' evolving thoughts and emotions. These interactions are pivotal as they not only provide emotional support but also reinforce the adolescents' sense of security and belonging.

The dialogue initiated by these questions also benefits the family unit. It encourages a culture of openness and trust, where young individuals feel valued and understood. In turn, this supports their social and emotional development, equipping them with the confidence to engage with the world around them more positively and assertively.

## Navigating Modern Challenges

Today's adolescents are growing up in a digitally interconnected world exposed to various influences, from global cultural trends to social media dynamics. The questions in this book are designed to help them critically assess the information and values they encounter online and in the media. By fostering discernment and encouraging them to question what they see and hear, we aid them in developing a grounded sense of self and a resilient moral compass.

Moreover, these questions address the unique pressures and issues faced by today's youth, such as mental health, academic stress, and future uncertainties. Through our questions, we can reassure them that they are not navigating these issues alone, while also empowering them to find their solutions and paths forward.

## A Call to Engage

As we embark on the journey through this book, it is my hope that the questions we explore together will serve as catalysts for growth and discovery. Each question is a stepping stone towards a deeper understanding and a stronger relationship with the young adolescents we care about so deeply. By dedicating time to engage with them through these inquiries, we are not only investing in their current well-being but also in their ability to thrive as adults.

Let this book be a testament to the power of questions, which, when asked with genuine curiosity and care, have the potential to transform lives. It is with great anticipation and hope that we step into this dialogue together, ready to inspire and be inspired.

Let the journey of questions begin.

Devon & Mauricio

# Share Your Experience

Thank you for choosing this book. We hope this has provided meaningful insights and fostered valuable conversations for you and your child.

Your feedback helps us improve and helps other parents and young readers discover this resource. Reviews increase the book's visibility, making it easier for those who might benefit from its content to find it.

If you found this book helpful, please take a moment to leave a review by scanning this QR code.

Your experience can inspire and guide others on their journey of self-discovery and growth. We appreciate your support. Thank you.

Devon & Mauricio

# Scan the QR code to access the full collection

# Disclaimer

Dear Readers,

This book is designed to serve as a tool for personal growth, reflection, and exploring thoughts and feelings. The questions provided within these pages aim to inspire introspection and conversation, fostering a deeper understanding of oneself and the world.

However, it is important to understand that this book is not a substitute for professional advice, diagnosis, or treatment. While the questions can guide meaningful discussions and self-discovery, they are not intended to address or resolve serious issues or health concerns.

If you or your child encounters significant emotional, psychological, or physical challenges, we strongly recommend seeking the guidance of a qualified professional. This may include consulting a doctor, mental health professional, counselor, or any other relevant specialist who can provide the appropriate support and interventions.

The publisher, author, and any associated parties take no responsibility for any consequences resulting from the use of this book. It is up to the reader to exercise their judgment and discretion when engaging with the questions and interpreting their answers. The insights and reflections gained from this book should be seen as a starting point for further exploration and, when necessary, professional consultation.

We hope that this book serves as a valuable resource for personal growth and development. Remember, each individual's journey of self-discovery is unique, and seeking help when needed is a sign of strength and wisdom.

# Guidelines for Asking Questions to Adolescents

Read the following guidelines to learn more about asking questions that unlock learning, foster communication and improve relationships.

- **Effective questions are open or focused, depending on the context**: Questions that open awareness and learning are open-ended questions that cannot be answered with a yes or no. Such questions evoke deeper thinking and reflection.

- **Effective questions support learning**: The goal is to stimulate thinking and deepen understanding of the situation. Insightful questions should focus attention on the most valuable aspects of the issue at hand, helping adolescents understand their experiences and feelings better.

- **Effective questions are asked for the benefit of others**: The intent is to stimulate the thinking and deepen the understanding of adolescents. It is not necessarily about the questioner and their needs.

- **Effective questions engage a personal response**: Engaging adolescents by inviting a personal response—how they feel, what emotions they are bringing to the situation—is crucial. The more a question invites a personal response to a challenge or choice, the more powerful it is for facilitating learning and growth.

- **Effective questions look beyond problems to future outcomes**: When adolescents are entangled in a problem, impactful questions shift the perspective from the problem to the solution, opening new opportunities for action and positive thinking.

- **Effective questions facilitate openness versus defensiveness**: Impactful questions are worded and expressed with a non-judgmental tone and open body language to prevent a defensive reaction. It is usually best to avoid questions that begin with "why" since they often elicit defensive responses or explanations

- **Effective questions co-create best options versus manipulating outcomes**: Impactful questions are not intended to manipulate or lead adolescents to the option you might think is the best. If you want to suggest, it is best made directly as a suggestion versus a disguised directive through a question.

- **Less is more**: For questions, less is usually more. Ask only one question at a time and avoid long-winded, complicated questions. A short, simple question—What is that all about? What will the consequences be?—pulls the respondent straight to the core.

## **<u>Day 1</u>**
What activities help you manage stress?

## **<u>Day 2</u>**
Have you noticed any new changes in your body recently, and how do you feel about them?

## **<u>Day 3</u>**
What does self-esteem mean to you, and what can you do to boost yours?

## **<u>Day 4</u>**
How do you usually express your feelings when you're upset?

## Day 5
What makes you feel appreciated and valued?

## Day 6
What qualities do you look for in a friend?

## Day 7
How important is it for you to fit in with your peers?

## Day 8
What subjects are you most interested in, and why?

## Day 9
What's a recent academic challenge you faced, and how did you handle it?

## Day 10
What does mental health mean to you, and why is it important?

## Day 11
What physical activities do you enjoy the most, and how do they make you feel afterward?

## Day 12
What's your favorite meal that you also consider healthy?

## Day 13
Who is someone you can talk to when you're feeling down?

## Day 14
How do you handle disagreements with your friends?

## Day 15
What are your thoughts on continuing education after high school?

## Day 16
What activities help you manage stress?

## Day 17
How does your cultural background influence your daily life?

## Day 18
What role does media play in your decisions and perceptions?

## Day 19
What makes you feel safe in your community?

## Day 20
How do you define your personal values?

## **Day 21**
What strategies do you use to cope with feeling unsafe?




## **Day 22**
How do you ensure your safety when you're online?




## **Day 23**
How does your environment (urban or rural) impact your lifestyle?




## **Day 24**
What are your favorite outdoor activities that connect you with nature?

## Day 25
What does honesty mean to you, and why is it important in relationships?

## Day 26
How much water do you drink daily, and do you think it's enough?

## Day 27
What steps can you take to improve your sleep habits for better health?

## Day 28
How does your physical health affect your daily activities and mood?

## Day 29
Can you describe a recent situation in which you managed your emotions well?

## Day 30
What qualities do you admire in yourself?

## Day 31
What role do your cultural traditions play in your life?

## Day 32
When you disagree with someone's opinion online, how do you respond?

## Day 33
How do you feel about the privacy settings on your social media accounts?

## Day 34
What steps do you take to maintain your physical health during stressful times?

## Day 35
What is one skill you'd like to improve this year?

## Day 36
How do you feel when you help someone else?

## Day 37
What do you think makes a teacher or coach influential?

## Day 38
How do you manage distractions when you need to focus on homework?

## Day 39
What are your strategies for dealing with criticism?

## Day 40
What aspect of your future career excites you the most?

## Day 41
How do you celebrate your achievements?

## Day 42
What are the most important lessons you've learned from your parents?

## Day 43
How do you handle feelings of jealousy or envy?

## Day 44
What is one tradition you cherish in your family?

## **Day 45**
How do you think traveling to different places impacts a person?

## **Day 46**
What book has significantly influenced your thinking?

## **Day 47**
How do you prioritize your mental health during exam periods?

## **Day 48**
What is one thing you'd change about your daily routine to improve your productivity?

## Day 49
How do you approach learning a new skill or hobby?

## Day 50
What does success in school mean to you?

## Day 51
How do you approach responsibilities at home?

## Day 52
What do you think is the key to maintaining strong friendships?

## Day 53
How do you feel about the amount of time you spend on digital devices?


## Day 54
What artistic or creative activities do you enjoy the most?


## Day 55
How do you react when things don't go as planned?


## Day 56
What are your thoughts on leadership? What makes a good leader?

## Day 57
How do you think being in nature affects you?

## Day 58
What are the most significant pressures teenagers face today?

## Day 59
How do you make decisions about spending and saving money?

## Day 60
What role does faith or spirituality play in your life?

## Day 61
How do you maintain a balance between online and in-person interactions?


## Day 62
What are your strategies for overcoming procrastination?


## Day 63
How do you stay informed about current events?


## Day 64
What does personal growth mean to you?

## Day 65
How do you feel about the responsibilities you're given at home?

## Day 66
What are your thoughts on climate change and environmental responsibility?

## Day 67
How do you express love and appreciation in your family?

## Day 68
What do you think is most challenging about growing up today?

## Day 69
How do you approach problem-solving in your personal life?

## Day 70
What are your views on teamwork in school and sports?

## Day 71
How do you deal with the expectations placed on you by others?

## Day 72
What strategies do you use to build your self-confidence?

## Day 73
How do you handle the stress of making important decisions about your future?

## Day 74
What are your goals for the next year?

## Day 75
How do you stay motivated when you face setbacks?

## Day 76
What are your thoughts on the importance of honesty in friendships?

## Day 77
What activities make you feel the most energized?


## Day 78
How do you think your experiences as a teenager will influence your adulthood?


## Day 79
In what ways do you think respecting others' differences is important?


## Day 80
How do you feel about asking for help when you need it?

## Day 81
What role does forgiveness play in your relationships?

## Day 82
How do you deal with the pressure to succeed academically?

## Day 83
What does being a good friend mean to you?

## Day 84
How do you balance your personal desires with your responsibilities?

## Day 85
What are the qualities you admire in your role models?

## Day 86
How do you define 'family'?

## Day 87
What's your approach to handling disagreements without escalating them?

## Day 88
How has your perspective on money and finances changed as you've grown older?

## Day 89
What are some ways you think young people can contribute to their communities?

## Day 90
How do you handle the stress of uncertainty about the future?

## Day 91
What are your strategies for maintaining focus during long tasks?

## Day 92
How do you approach making new friends?

### Day 93
What are the most challenging aspects of your school life?

### Day 94
How do you prioritize your wellness in a busy schedule?

### Day 95
What experiences have taught you the most about yourself?

### Day 96
How do you respond to change?

## Day 97
What are your thoughts on the importance of privacy?

## Day 98
How do you think being a teenager today is different because of technology?

## Day 99
What steps do you take to improve a bad day?

## Day 100
How do you celebrate your personal achievements?

## Day 101
What's the most important thing you've learned about relationships?

## Day 102
How do you handle feelings of loneliness or isolation?

## Day 103
What do you look forward to the most each week?

## Day 104
How do you prepare for important tests or presentations?

## **Day 105**
What are your favorite ways to relax and unwind?

## **Day 106**
How do you approach resolving misunderstandings with others?

## **Day 107**
What kind of support do you find most helpful when you're struggling?

## **Day 108**
How do you deal with setbacks in sports or other extracurricular activities?

## Day 109
What are your views on discipline and self-control?

## Day 110
How do you feel about your role in your peer group?

## Day 111
What are your thoughts on global issues like climate change or human rights?

## Day 112
How do you define success in personal terms?

## Day 113
What new skill would you like to learn this year?


## Day 114
How do you manage your emotions during competitive situations?


## Day 115
What has been the biggest challenge in your relationships with peers?


## Day 116
How do you approach conversations about difficult topics with your parents?

## Day 117
What are the top three values you try to live by?

## Day 118
How do you make decisions about using social media responsibly?

## Day 119
What are the benefits of teamwork, in your experience?

## Day 120
How do you feel about your impact on others?

## Day 121
What goals do you have for your physical health?

## Day 122
How do you express creativity in your daily life?

## Day 123
What are your strategies for dealing with rejection or failure?

## Day 124
How do you think about balancing independence with family expectations?

## Day 125
What are the things that make you feel most fulfilled?

## Day 126
How do you prepare for major life changes, like going to college or starting a job?

## Day 127
What steps do you take to respect others' boundaries?

## Day 128
How do you deal with peer influence when it conflicts with your values?

## Day 129
What are your thoughts on taking leadership roles?

## Day 130
How do you prioritize tasks when everything seems urgent?

## Day 131
What strategies do you find effective for managing stress before an important event?

## Day 132
How do you stay connected with friends in a meaningful way?

## Day 133
What does it mean to you to be responsible?

## Day 134
How do you approach learning from your mistakes?

## Day 135
What has been your most memorable experience this year?

## Day 136
How do you define a healthy relationship?

## Day 137
What is one thing you wish you could change about the world?

## Day 138
How do you approach discussions on sensitive topics with your peers?

## Day 139
What are your views on personal accountability?

## Day 140
How do you celebrate successes with your friends?

## Day 141
What are your methods for overcoming distractions while studying?


## Day 142
How do you respond to constructive feedback?


## Day 143
In what ways do you contribute to your family's well-being?


## Day 144
How do you decide what is right or wrong in complex situations?

## Day 145
What role does intuition play in your decision-making process?

## Day 146
How do you approach setting and achieving personal goals?

## Day 147
What are the key factors that make you feel fulfilled in a hobby or activity?

## Day 148
How do you handle competing demands from school, friends, and family?

## Day 149
What have you learned about yourself from a recent challenge?

## Day 150
How do you ensure you are listening actively when someone is speaking to you?

## Day 151
What are your strategies for maintaining your physical and mental well-being?

## Day 152
How do you handle situations where you feel out of your comfort zone?

## Day 153
What inspires you to be your best self?

## Day 154
How do you deal with feelings of inadequacy or self-doubt?

## Day 155
What do you think is the most important trait a leader should have?

## Day 156
How do you make time for yourself despite a busy schedule?

## Day 157
What changes have you made this year that you are proud of?

## Day 158
How do you handle the pressures of social expectations?

## Day 159
What are your thoughts on the importance of tradition and culture in your life?

## Day 160
How do you approach balancing personal interests with academic or career obligations?

## Day 161
What steps do you take to cultivate patience in difficult situations?

## Day 162
How do you celebrate cultural events with your family or community?

## Day 163
What role does technology play in your education and personal growth?

## Day 164
How do you handle disagreements with people you respect?

## Day 165
What are your thoughts on the impact of global connectivity on personal relationships?

## Day 166
How do you manage your responsibilities to ensure nothing is overlooked?

## Day 167
What lessons have you learned from a personal failure?

## Day 168
How do you approach solving problems that seem insurmountable?

## Day 169
What are your coping mechanisms for handling unexpected challenges?

## Day 170
How do you maintain a sense of community in your life?

## Day 171
What motivates you to learn about new subjects or skills?

## Day 172
How do you approach conversations about future plans and aspirations?

## Day 173
What steps do you take to strengthen your resilience?

## Day 174
How do you approach taking care of your mental health?

## Day 175
What ways do you find most effective for managing time when juggling school and personal interests?

## Day 176
How do you approach making new acquaintances into close friends?

## Day 177
What aspects of your life give you the most happiness?

## Day 178
How do you think volunteering or helping others impacts your personal growth?

## Day 179
What role does physical exercise play in your mental wellbeing?

## Day 180
How do you find balance between online and offline activities?

## Day 181
What are your methods for dealing with rejection in friendships or relationships?


## Day 182
How do you handle the stress of important decisions about your future, like college or career paths?


## Day 183
What are your thoughts on the ethics of everyday decisions, like consumption or media choices?


## Day 184
How do you express your individuality through your hobbies or interests?

## Day 185
What experiences have shaped your views on personal freedom and independence?

## Day 186
How do you deal with conflicts that arise within your family?

## Day 187
What do you think are the keys to sustaining long-term friendships?

## Day 188
How do you approach learning from different cultures or perspectives?

## Day 189
What strategies do you use to boost your self-esteem when you feel low?

## Day 190
How do you decide when it's necessary to compromise with others?

## Day 191
What are your views on the importance of community service in shaping character?

## Day 192
How do you maintain motivation when you're not seeing immediate results from your efforts?

## Day 193
What role does creativity play in your personal development?

## Day 194
How do you approach discussions about sensitive or controversial topics?

## Day 195
What are the most important factors you consider when planning for your future?

## Day 196
How do you determine the credibility of the information you receive, especially online?

## Day 197
What are your strategies for coping with overwhelming situations?

## Day 198
How do you build trust in new relationships?

## Day 199
What personal achievements are you most proud of this year?

## Day 200
How do you react to unexpected changes or disruptions to your plans?

## Day 201
How do you approach maintaining your privacy in digital spaces?

## Day 202
What lessons have you learned from a significant mistake?

## Day 203
How do you handle the balance between school responsibilities and personal life?

## Day 204
What are your thoughts on the impact of social media on self-image?

## Day 205
How do you stay true to your values in peer-pressure situations?

## Day 206
What are your strategies for dealing with loneliness or isolation?

## Day 207
How do you manage the stress of competitive environments, whether in sports or academics?

## Day 208
How do you cultivate a positive outlook in challenging circumstances?

## Day 209
What are the most valuable life lessons you have learned from your family?

## Day 210
How do you plan to achieve your current goals in the next year?

## Day 211
What ways do you seek to understand viewpoints different from your own?

## Day 212
How do you approach setting personal boundaries in relationships?

## Day 213
What has been your biggest challenge in developing self-discipline?

## Day 214
How do you deal with the pressure of achieving academic success?

## Day 215
What role does gratitude play in your daily life?

## Day 216
How do you think your life differs from that of your parents when they were your age?

## Day 217
What personal values do you think are most important for your future success?

## Day 218
How do you decide what aspects of your life to share on social media?

## Day 219
What strategies do you employ to improve your decision-making skills?

## Day 220
How do you handle feelings of insecurity or doubt about your abilities?

## Day 221
What are your methods for staying engaged in subjects you find challenging or uninteresting?

## Day 222
How do you approach responsibility, both personally and within your family?

## Day 223
What do you consider the most important aspect of maintaining good mental health?

## Day 224
How do you prepare for leadership roles, in school or other activities?

## Day 225
What new hobby or activity are you interested in trying, and why?

## Day 226
How do you think your friendships influence your decisions?

## Day 227
What do you value most in your closest relationships?

## Day 228
How do you approach forgiving someone who has hurt you?

## Day 229
What strategies do you use to manage stress from schoolwork?

## Day 230
How do you assess the risks and benefits before making a significant decision?

## Day 231
What steps have you taken to build or maintain physical fitness?

## Day 232
How do you nurture your mental health during challenging times?

## Day 233
What are your strategies for balancing social life and academic responsibilities?

## Day 234
How do you deal with the pressure to conform to social norms?

## Day 235
How do you react when you encounter failure in something important to you?

## Day 236
What do you think are the most critical factors in building a successful future?

### Day 237
How do you maintain your focus when faced with distractions?

### Day 238
What has been the most significant change in your life this past year?

### Day 239
How do you determine what makes someone a trustworthy friend?

### Day 240
How do you deal with criticism, whether constructive or unfair?

## Day 241
What aspects of your life do you think require more attention or improvement?

## Day 242
How do you manage your time when you have conflicting priorities?

## Day 243
What role does reflection play in your personal growth?

## Day 244
How do you handle conflicts with people who have different beliefs?

## Day 245
What are your thoughts on the role of technology in personal relationships?

## Day 246
How do you approach problem-solving in everyday challenges?

## Day 247
What do you do to ensure you're making the most out of your educational opportunities?

## Day 248
What kind of support do you find most beneficial from your family?

## Day 249
How do you handle situations where you feel misunderstood by others?

## Day 250
How do you approach maintaining a healthy lifestyle?

## Day 251
What steps do you take to ensure that you remain open-minded?

## Day 252
How do you prioritize your responsibilities and hobbies?

## Day 253
What have you learned about yourself from a recent experience?

## Day 254
How do you handle the pressure of social expectations?

## Day 255
What are the most important lessons you've learned about personal responsibility?

## Day 256
How do you approach repairing a friendship after a disagreement?

## Day 257
What role do you think gratitude plays in your life?

## Day 258
How do you define and pursue happiness?

## Day 259
What are your strategies for dealing with change, especially when unexpected?

## Day 260
How do you feel about your future, and what steps are you taking to prepare for it?

## Day 261
How do you think self-awareness contributes to your personal development?

## Day 262
What qualities do you believe make a strong leader?

## Day 263
How do you evaluate your own growth and progress over time?

## Day 264
What do you find most challenging about maintaining friendships?

## Day 265
How do you balance your personal interests with the demands of your education?

## Day 266
How do you approach learning from people who are different from you?

## Day 267
What actions do you take to stay safe online and in your daily life?

## Day 268
How do you manage feelings of frustration or anger?

## Day 269
What do you think about the balance between individual freedom and community responsibility?

## Day 270
How do you approach setting realistic goals for yourself?

## Day 271
What strategies do you employ to stay motivated, especially when tasks are challenging or tedious?

## Day 272
How do you decide whom to trust with personal issues?

## Day 273
What are your thoughts on the importance of self-expression?

## Day 274
How do you approach making amends when you've made a mistake?

## Day 275
How do you determine your personal strengths and how can you use them?

## Day 276
What are some ways you can help support your friends in tough times?

## Day 277
How do you balance the need for personal space with family expectations?

## Day 278
What are your thoughts on taking risks and stepping out of your comfort zone?

## Day 279
How do you decide which hobbies or activities to pursue seriously?

## Day 280
What measures do you take to manage and reduce stress in your life?

### Day 281
How do you approach setting boundaries in your personal and digital interactions?

### Day 282
What are the most effective ways you've found to improve your concentration and focus?

### Day 283
How do you handle moments of self-doubt and insecurity?

### Day 284
What steps do you take to cultivate a positive self-image?

## Day 285
How do you deal with the expectation to always "be strong" or not show vulnerability?

## Day 286
What does personal success look like to you, and how do you plan to achieve it?

## Day 287
How do you respond to changes in friendships as you grow older?

## Day 288
What are your thoughts on the impact of social norms on personal choices?

## Day 289
How do you stay informed about issues that are important to you?

## Day 290
What are your strategies for managing time effectively?

## Day 291
How do you decide what is most important when making decisions about the future?

## Day 292
How do you approach challenges that seem overwhelming?

## Day 293
What role does reflection play in your daily life?

## Day 294
How do you maintain motivation when your interests or goals change?

## Day 295
What actions do you take to ensure you're respecting others' views and feelings?

## Day 296
How do you handle feelings of competition with peers?

### Day 297
What are some ways you've found effective for expressing your thoughts and feelings?

### Day 298
How do you prioritize your health and wellbeing among school and social activities?

### Day 299
What has been your most transformative experience in the last year?

### Day 300
How do you approach learning from your failures?

## Day 301
What strategies do you use to build and maintain strong family relationships?

## Day 302
How do you approach problem-solving in group settings or team projects?

## Day 303
What are your thoughts on the role of discipline in personal growth?

## Day 304
How do you handle situations where you need to advocate for yourself?

### Day 305

How do you approach maintaining friendships with people who have different beliefs or lifestyles?

### Day 306

What are your thoughts on the importance of mentorship?

### Day 307

How do you manage the balance between achieving your goals and taking time to relax?

### Day 308

What are the biggest influences on your decision-making processes?

## Day 309
How do you stay motivated and engaged in subjects that are not your strongest?

## Day 310
What are your thoughts on the role of art and culture in personal development?

## Day 311
How do you determine the values that are most important to you?

## Day 312
What methods do you use to cope with anxiety or depression?

## Day 313
How do you handle the pressure of social media and its impact on your self-esteem?

## Day 314
What are your strategies for resolving conflicts without escalating them?

## Day 315
How do you ensure you are making thoughtful and informed decisions?

## Day 316
What steps do you take to develop leadership skills?

## Day 317
How do you approach discussing difficult topics with your peers?

## Day 318
What are your thoughts on the balance between privacy and openness in relationships?

## Day 319
How do you assess the role of technology in your daily life and learning?

## Day 320
What strategies do you use to encourage yourself to try new things?

## Day 321
How do you manage the expectations placed upon you by others?

## Day 322
What are your strategies for dealing with uncertainty about the future?

## Day 323
How do you evaluate the advice you receive from others?

## Day 324
What are your thoughts on the importance of community involvement?

## Day 325
How do you recognize when you need a break from technology?

## Day 326
What methods do you find effective for learning new skills or subjects quickly?

## Day 327
How do you deal with the pressure to excel in every area of your life?

## Day 328
What role does creativity play in your personal and academic life?

## Day 329
How do you determine which friendships are worth nurturing?

## Day 330
What practices help you stay grounded when you feel overwhelmed?

## Day 331
How do you handle conflicts that arise from misunderstandings?

## Day 332
What activities do you engage in that help you feel connected to your community?

## Day 333
How do you balance your personal aspirations with your family's expectations?

## Day 334
What steps do you take to maintain a healthy lifestyle despite a busy schedule?

## Day 335
How do you approach making decisions that have long-term implications?

## Day 336
What techniques do you use to cope with anxiety or nervousness in social situations?

## Day 337
How do you approach maintaining your personal values in various social settings?

## Day 338
What challenges have you faced in maintaining your physical health, and how have you addressed them?

## Day 339
How do you prioritize tasks and projects to ensure you meet deadlines?

## Day 340
What has been a significant learning moment for you this year, and why?

## Day 341
How do you approach forgiveness, both in offering it to others and seeking it for yourself?

## Day 342
What are your thoughts on the influence of peer pressure in decision-making?

## Day 343
How do you define personal integrity, and how do you strive to uphold it?

## Day 344
What steps do you take to be more mindful and present in your daily activities?

## Day 345
How do you handle situations where you feel out of place or uncomfortable?

## Day 346
What strategies do you employ to improve your communication skills?

## Day 347
How do you manage your responsibilities to optimize your academic performance?

## Day 348
What role do hobbies and leisure activities play in your mental health?

## Day 349
How do you approach setting realistic and achievable goals?

## Day 350
What are your strategies for dealing with criticism from peers or teachers?

## Day 351
How do you balance the need for independence with the benefits of guidance from adults?

## Day 352
What are the most important factors you consider when planning your career or future studies?

## Day 353
How do you manage the stress of competitive environments, such as sports or academic contests?

## Day 354
What actions do you take to build resilience in the face of setbacks?

## Day 355
How do you ensure you are respectful of different cultural perspectives?

## Day 356
What methods do you use to stay organized and efficient?

## Day 357
How do you determine the trustworthiness of information you find online?

## Day 358
What are your thoughts on the importance of self-care, and how do you practice it?

## Day 359
How do you deal with feelings of inadequacy or comparison to others?

## Day 360
What strategies do you find most helpful in maintaining a positive outlook?

## Day 361
How do you handle the transition from high school to further education or the workforce?

## Day 362
What steps do you take to strengthen your decision-making skills?

## Day 363
How do you manage the balance between your personal and academic life?

## Day 364
What have you learned about yourself from group projects or teamwork?

## Day 365

How do you reflect on your growth over the past year, and what goals do you have for the next year?

# Share Your Experience

Thank you for choosing this book. We hope this has provided meaningful insights and fostered valuable conversations for you and your child.

Your feedback helps us improve and helps other parents and young readers discover this resource. Reviews increase the book's visibility, making it easier for those who might benefit from its content to find it.

If you found this book helpful, please take a moment to leave a review by scanning this QR code.

Your experience can inspire and guide others on their journey of self-discovery and growth. We appreciate your support. Thank you.

Devon & Mauricio

www.ingramcontent.com/pod-product-compliance
Lightning Source LLC
Chambersburg PA
CBHW081337120626
46546CB00011B/3393